3 8002 01235 9909

D0492961

blend me,
shake me!
101 hip new cocktails

Written by
Alex Kammerling

Photography by
Martin Langfield

I would like to dedicate this book to my new baby girl. Unfortunately, you will have to wait 18 years before you can fully appreciate it. AK

Published by BBC Books, BBC Worldwide Ltd, Woodlands,
80 Wood Lane, London W12 0TT

First published 2004 by BBC Books

ISBN 0563 48795 X

Commissioning Editor: Vivien Bowler
Project Editor: Yvonne Bristow
Project Editor for BBC Books: Helena Caldon
Jacket Art Director: Pene Parker
Book design: hat-trick design consultants
Production Controller: Arlene Alexander

Set in Shaker, a Jeremy Tankard typeface
Printed and bound in Singapore by Tien Wah Press
Colour separations by Radstock Reproductions, Midsomer Norton

There are many brands of alcoholic drinks available. The brands recommended by the author are his personal favourites.

For more information about this and other BBC books, please visit our website on www.bbcshop.com

Warning:
I hope that you like the recipes in this book, and while drinking in moderation is fine, please remember that alcohol is a drug and should not be abused. Excessive use of alcohol can lead to addiction and all kinds of nasty repercussions and illness. If you have to drive or operate heavy machinery, stick to the non-alcoholic drinks at the back of this book. AK

Contents

In relation to human history, the production and consumption of spirits is a new concept. This means that metaphorically speaking, cocktail culture is still a kicking, screaming baby. We do not know when the first cocktail was born, but various nations have been mixing their drinks for hundreds of years and many of today's classic cocktails were created before the word 'cocktail' was even being used.

Cocktail culture as we know it today really started in America in 1919 with the era of Prohibition. This began when the manufacture, sale and transportation of alcohol was declared illegal. President Herbert Hoover described Prohibition as a noble experiment, designed to reduce the consumption of alcohol by Americans, which reformers believed was reaching alarmingly high levels.

All that happened was that drinking culture went underground, to the speakeasies, where the only available alcohol was illegally smuggled moonshine, a trade controlled by gangsters such as Al Capone. This alcohol was such bad quality that it needed lots of sugar, bitters and vermouth to make it palatable. Cocktails were born.

During the Prohibition era, which lasted for more than a decade, many Americans (including bartenders) travelled to Cuba, England, Paris and Italy spreading their ideas and cocktail knowledge. This helped inspire the world and soon enough, the cocktail floodgates opened. Prohibition was repealed by President Franklin D. Roosevelt in 1933, when America was in the throes of a depression. People needed a release from the general malaise and a new style of escapism emerged in the form of Polynesian Pop, or Tiki Culture. Strong, fruity rum-based drinks such as the Mai Tai and the Zombie were created by legendary bartenders such as Trader Vic and Don the Beachcomber, and when American GIs came back from fighting in the South Pacific during World War Two, they brought with them stories of white beaches, beautiful women and exotic culture. Enthusiasm for all things tropical was fuelled by Hawaii joining the union in 1959 and films such as *South Pacific* and, of course, *Blue Hawaii*, which starred Elvis.

The era that is best left in the cocktail closet however is the Eighties. Tom Cruise may have been a good juggler and a lady killer in the film *Cocktail*, but he managed to forget one small but crucial point – that cocktails are for drinking, they are not about showing off.

All manner of excessive drinks were created during this period including layered and coloured shooters, Flaming Lamborghinis and blended ice-cream drinks. We have emerged from the last century more mature and a lot wiser. Many of the drinks that were created in these times have fallen by the wayside and only the greats have survived.

Apart from the classics, all the recipes in this book are new, sophisticated inventions. I have tried to create a range of drinks which will appeal to a cross section of tastes and although you will like most of the drinks here, you might not like all of them.

My aim in writing this book is to broaden people's horizons and push cocktail culture on a little. I hope that, in the course of working your way through this book, you will find at least one that you will drink regularly. Better still, I hope that this book blows away the cobwebs of previous cocktail books and will inspire you to create your own drinks.

So what is the point of a cocktail? According to David Embury, a famous alcohol aficionado from the 1950s:

> 'The well-made cocktail is one of the most gracious drinks...the shared delight of those who partake in common of this refreshing nectar breaks the ice of formal reserve. Taut nerves relax; taut muscles relax; tired eyes brighten; tongues loosen; friendships deepen; the whole world becomes a better place in which to live.'

Just like a good meal, a good drink should taste great and be true to its ingredients. For me, a cocktail is a different way in which to enjoy spirits. The flavour of the main (or base) spirit should be clear to the palate, but not over-powering. The mixers help bring out the hidden personality of the spirit by complementing certain characteristics within the taste. A cocktail should be appealing to the eye – and most importantly, it should be moreish.

Five Basic Principles at the Heart of a Great Cocktail:

1/ Balance
Getting the proportions right between the ingredients – whether sweet, sour, dry, bitter or creamy – is the primary concern when making a cocktail. At the beginning of the book I've given a recipe for Old-fashioned Lemonade. It is easy to make, but by getting the correct balance of sweet and sour, you will turn an OK drink into a fantastic one.

2/ Dilution
Most cocktails rely on ice to chill them – but the wrong kind of ice, or the right kind of ice used in the wrong way, can turn a good drink bad. Basically, you want to keep as much of the flavour in the drink as possible. By allowing ice to melt in your drink, you are watering down this flavour.

When a recipe tells you to 'shake a drink with ice', you should add the cubes last of all. Put all the ingredients into a shaker, then fill it right up with ice and shake the drink vigorously for a few seconds to get it as cold as possible as quickly as possible. Once the drink is icy cold, strain it into a glass filled with fresh ice and discard the ice in the shaker – this will ensure that your drink stays fresh and cold for longer.

If you are going to make a number of cocktails in an evening, then forget about those silly plastic ice-cube trays. Small ice cubes melt too quickly and water down your drink – if you have very chlorinated tap water, you'll also be able to taste it. Buy a bag of ice that has good chunky cubes (normally, they are UV-filtered which means that they are also clear). When you shake the drink it should make a loud, clattering noise, not a quiet, slushy one.

3/ Strength
Make sure your drink tastes of the main ingredient – the booze! You hear some people say, 'That's nice, you can't even taste the alcohol.' Well, a good cocktail should taste of alcohol (vodka aside). A cocktail should bring out the personality of the spirit, but not let it overpower the mix. On the other hand, people are tempted to chuck half a bottle into a drink at parties. Although this may speed up the party atmosphere, it kills any subtle flavours and lingering enjoyment. As a general rule, most drinks including mixers have a 'firm but fair' double measure (50 ml/1.5 fl oz) of standard (40% ABV/80% proof) spirit.

4/ Ingredients
As with most things, the final product is only as good as the sum of its parts. A cocktail made with reconstituted fruit juice and cheap spirits is not going to be half as good as one crafted from premium brands and freshly squeezed, sun-ripened fruit. It is, of course, more expensive and time consuming to use these things: that's life – you get what you pay for.

5/ The serve
Making your drinks look appealing to the eye is essential. This means using the right-shaped glass, filling the glass up properly and garnishing your drinks. You can, of course, serve any drink in any glass, but serving a Martini in a pint glass is like eating fillet steak from a plastic bowl. Some glasses are designed to sip from, others for thirst quenching and others for shooting. The shape of the glass is also highly evocative and changes the way you hold and drink the cocktail. Garnishing drinks is an added extra. Some drinks don't need garnishing, but those that do should be garnished with an ingredient that is used within the cocktail. (For more tips on garnishing see 'How to' on page 110.)

The simple shape of the martini glass is a design classic. It holds a small volume of (usually) very potent cocktail. If you grab a martini like you would a pint of beer, you'll find yourself wearing it. The martini glass is a model of sophistication and has to be treated with sensitivity and respect – as it was by James Bond and Frank Sinatra.

The tumbler is a personal favourite – whether you call it a rocks glass, an old-fashioned or just a plain old tumbler. Its weight and size fit comfortably into the hand; it holds a healthy amount of alcohol (there's an oxymoron). Filled with spirits over ice, it makes a fantastically pleasing noise, and it is also hard to spill or knock over.

This is the regulation highball glass – or Collins if you prefer. Filled to the brim, it will hold 300 ml/10 fl oz/½ pint (nearly a bottle of beer) and is ideal for most occasions. That said, there is a huge difference in the quality of these glasses. It is pointless to make a stunning drink and serve it in a glass which you got as a free offer, when you could serve it in a crystal glass with a good solid base and a nicely finished edge.

This elegant number is, of course, a champagne flute. It works much better than the old, saucer-shaped glass as it keeps in more of the fizz (although you can't make a champagne fountain from these glasses).

The shot glass. Every home should have at least four. They come in various sizes – 25 ml/1 fl oz is a standard 'shot' as you would get it in a bar, although some of the designer ones are not even standard measures. Shot glasses also come in double measures (holding 50 ml/1.5 fl oz) and can be used to measure ingredients for longer drinks.

The 'mmm' test

My own taste scale and the ethos of cocktail-making in this book is what I call the 'mmm' test. Great flavours, whether in food or drink, make us screw up our eyes with appreciation and we find ourselves making the (almost cow-like) 'mmm' noise, which is a sign of moreishness. You haven't made a good drink until you get the 'mmm' factor – the more 'mmms', the merrier!

Tip 1 Cocktails taste better from sparkling clean glasses. If you put your glasses through a dishwasher, make sure to use rinse aid. If you don't, use dishwasher rinse aid in your washing up bowl – it helps the water run off them and reduces water marks. (See tip 10 on page 87 for glass polishing tips.)

Equipment

Blender

If you do not own one, there will be a handful of drinks in this book which you will not be able to make. If you are thinking of buying one, then get the most powerful blender that you can afford. Ideally, it should have a number of speed settings (including 'pulse') and sturdy blades which are capable of crushing ice. A solid glass blender jug is the best so that you can monitor the colour and amount of liquid you put in. Before you part with cash, also check that the top has a good rubber seal.

Measure

In this book, I have listed recipes in millilitres (ml) and fluid ounces (fl oz) and tried to round up/down the measurements to divisions of 25 ml (1 fl oz). Professional bars use stainless steel measures, known as jiggers, but you can substitute an egg cup, an old film case, a shot glass, a medicine measure, the cap from a bottle – anything. Just make sure that you work out how many millilitres it holds (you'll need maths and a measuring jug) before letting rip. (See conversion table on page 117 for details.)

Rolling pin

Ideal for smashing ice, crushing fresh fruits, rolling pastry and playing indoor baseball.

Lemon squeezer

A flashy one is normally better than a cheap one, but all the juice I ever squeeze comes from these glass ones.

Sieve

Very important for straining off mint leaves or raspberry pips that might otherwise get stuck in your teeth.

Shaker
Don't invest in anything that costs less than a good bottle of gin – it will leak. Of course, an empty jar and a plastic container are equally good, but you won't look as cool. I personally prefer clear shakers (so that you can monitor the amount and colour of the drink); these metal ones are easy to use and better for judging the temperature of the drink when shaking (when the cold hurts your hands, it is ready).

Sharp knife
No cocktail guru should be without one.

Potato peeler
Use this to peel the skin off lemons, limes and oranges (for infusions and for zesting).

Spoons
All you will need is a standard teaspoon (5 ml) and a tablespoon (15 ml) for measuring sugar and small amounts of liquid.

Measuring jug
Essential for measuring large amounts of liquid. For details on measurements and conversions, go to the conversion table on page 117.

Other things that are always good to have to hand are nibbles, lots of friends and large quantities of good-quality alcohol.

Booze – the basics

As I mentioned earlier, the final product is only as good as the sum of its parts. Try not to skimp on the quality of the ingredients, especially not the spirit. Cheap spirits have a harsh burn to them, do not have the same depth of flavour and are far more likely to give you a stonking hangover! Here is a selection of personal favourites that mix well into cocktails.

Vodka

Vodka can be made from numerous raw ingredients – including molasses, potatoes and even onions. However, the better vodkas are produced from grain such as wheat or rye and then mixed with pure spring or glacial waters. Some are then filtered through charcoal or sand to purify them even further. My personal choice of vodkas is the original Russian Stolichnaya which is made from winter wheat – it is clean, crisp and fresh and makes a good base for cocktails as well as being fantastic in Martinis.

'There is no ugliness, only too little vodka.'
Old Russian proverb

Brandy

Brandy can be made from any fruit – but most brandies are made from grapes. Unless otherwise stated the recipes in this book use Cognac which is an exclusive style of grape brandy made only in the Cognac region of France. Cognac is special due to the fantastic soil the grapes are grown in as well as a dedicated and refined production process used to distill and age the Cognac. Martell VS is an excellent Cognac for all round mixing as it is rich and smooth with a well balanced fruitiness.

Tequila

Tequila is made from a large spiky plant called the Agave. This plant thrives in the volcanic soils of Mexico, which is why in the indigenous tribes' language 'Tequila' translates as 'lava hill'. Tequilas that are made from 100% Agave are the best like this brand which is called Gran Centenario. Look for 'Añejo' or 'Reposado' on the label, which means the tequila has been 'aged' or 'rested' in wood. This is the 'Plata' or 'white' version and is an excellent style of Tequila for cocktails. It is very smooth, has a good fruitiness and a little peppery spice on the finish.

Rum

In 1655, when the British Navy took Jamaica from the Spaniards, they found stocks of a strong spirit made from sugar cane – later termed rum. Naturally, they started giving their sailors half a pint of it a day. The rum was mixed with lime juice to ward off scurvy, which is why the Brits are known as 'limeys'. Buy golden rums that have been aged – they are much smoother and fuller flavoured than clear rums, which can be a bit harsh. Appleton Estate V/X Jamaica rum is my personal choice for all round mixing as it is rich and mellow and mixes perfectly in cocktails.

Whisky

Whisky is made all over the world, but the fantastic natural resources, climate and experience in Scotland means that it produces its own superior styles. For cocktails, try and buy a blended whisky (referred to as 'Scotch') which contains a mixture of single malts and grain whiskies from the different regions of Scotland. Chivas Regal is a fine example of a blend and a personal favourite of mine. At the heart of Chivas are malt whiskies produced in Speyside, giving it a rich, honeyed, floral nose with a long smooth finish – making it ideal for cocktails.

'I never drink anything stronger than gin before breakfast.' *W.C. Fields*

Gin

Once termed 'mother's ruin' due to the alcoholism of imbibing working class mums during the industrial revolution in Great Britain, there are now numerous high quality gins. Gin is essentially vodka flavoured with herbs and spices – good gins balance the distinctive tang of juniper with other additions such as coriander, cinnamon, liquorice and citrus peel. I favour Plymouth gin which is made in England's oldest working distillery. It is less juniper heavy than London Dry Gins and makes a perfect base for all the gin-based drinks in this book.

Liqueurs

Liqueurs are sweetened, flavoured spirits and are generally less alcoholic than the other spirit categories. Their flavour can come from anything, fruits, nuts, herbs, roots, orange peel, honey or even flowers. French and Italian liqueurs are generally better than the Dutch ones as they tend to have a fuller, fresher taste. The main liqueur in this book is the French orange liqueur Grand Marnier. It is made from bitter orange peels from the Caribbean and uses cognac as a base which gives cocktails additional depth and structure as well as providing a richer, smoother taste.

Bourbon

Bourbon is 'American whiskey'. Unlike Scotch, it is distilled from corn and other grain (but not malted barley). The distinctive woody, vanilla flavour from bourbon comes from the oak barrels in which it is aged. The insides of the barrels are burnt and this helps the whiskey to mature. (Legally, the barrels are only allowed to be used once and a lot of them are bought by Scottish distilleries for ageing single malt.) My personal favourite, and the one I recommend, is Wild Turkey 8 year old (101 proof). Its well-balanced, smooth character makes it ideal for drinking neat or mixing into cocktails.

This is the easiest and the hardest drink in this book to make and is a great illustration of how to 'balance' a cocktail. For me, this drink is the cornerstone of cocktail making. If you understand and can control the relationship between sweet, sour, dilution and alcoholic strength, then you are halfway to becoming a cocktail Jedi.

Old-fashioned lemonade

Serves 1

juice of 1 lemon
2 tbsp (30 ml) caster sugar
chilled sparkling mineral water (or soda water)

Pour the lemon juice into a highball glass, add the sugar and stir well until dissolved. Add ice and top up the glass with chilled fizzy water – that's it!

This lemonade should be sweet *and* sour. It should be refreshing and leave a long tangy puckering in your mouth. If it's too watery, too acidic or too sweet for your palate, add more sugar, lemon juice or water until you think it is right. When I was taught about making cocktails I was told that a drink is right when it tastes good to *you*.

You can now slug a bit of vodka or gin in it (which turns it into a 'vodka Collins' or a 'Tom Collins', depending which spirit you use). This will change the balance – you will need at least another teaspoon of sugar to get the balance right again but the results should be almost the same – refreshing and tangy, but with the kick of alcohol.

All the recipes in this book are tailored to my own palate. At the end of the day, you are the person making and drinking them and you may want to sweeten or sour the recipes to your own taste.

'For no certain weight can be mentioned, as the acidity of a lemon cannot be known till tried and therefore this must be determined by the taste.' *Jerry Thomas, 1862 (the world's first bartender)*

A sense of occasion

It has often been said that it is not an occasion unless you have a drink. The drinks in this chapter are designed for all kinds of celebrations, from simple get-togethers to all-out social shenanigans.

This is one of my all-time faves. It originated in Cuba around the turn of the last century and has a great combination of flavours. Made right, it is simple perfection.

Here is a twist on the traditional Bloody Mary – perfect for a balmy summer afternoon with a burnt steak. (Liquid smoke is found in the section of the supermarket where all the marinades are sold.)

Mojito (classic)

Serves 1

50 ml/1.5 fl oz aged rum
8 fresh mint leaves (plus 1 sprig of mint for garnish)
2–3 tsp soft brown sugar
1 lime, cut into 6 wedges

In a tumbler or highball glass, crush the mint, sugar and sliced lime with a blunt tool such as a pestle, the end of a rolling pin or the handle of a wooden spoon. When the juice from the lime has been extracted and the sugar has dissolved, fill the glass almost to the brim with crushed ice. Slug in the rum, stir well and serve garnished with a sprig of mint.

Bloody Mary-Lou

Serves 4

200 ml/7 fl oz bourbon
1 litre/32 fl oz tomato juice
50 ml/1.5 fl oz liquid smoke
juice of 2 lemons
pinch of salt
pinch of pepper
1 lemon, cut into eight
4 spring onions, trimmed

Mix the first six ingredients well in a large jug. Stir in some ice cubes and the lemon wedges and serve at leisure. Use the spring onions to stir the drinks with and to munch on.

Don't let poor-quality fizz spoil the celebrations. This can be made with anything bubbly, although champagne is always best.

You may have been wondering what the hell you were going to do with both those bottles of advocaat and sherry sitting in your fridge – here is the answer! A great little after-dinner drink – dry and tangy, but strangely smooth and creamy.

Rosso Royale
Serves 1

25 ml/1 fl oz sweet red vermouth
½ tsp caster sugar
25 ml/1 fl oz cranberry juice
something bubbly
fresh cranberries for garnish (optional)

Place the sugar in the bottom of a champagne flute. Pour over the vermouth and cranberry juice, then gently fill with the bubbly of your choice. Throw in a few cranberries for decoration if you wish.

Canary
Serves 2

100 ml/3.5 fl oz advocaat
100 ml/3.5 fl oz dry sherry
½ lemon

Peel two strips of lemon peel first, then squeeze the lemon. Throw the juice and the alcohol into a cocktail shaker with some ice and shake hard. Strain into martini glasses and use the lemon peel to zest the surface of the cocktail. (For details on 'zesting' see page 116).

> **Tip 2** When shaking drinks, make sure that the shaker is packed full of ice and shake it using a few bursts of short, hard shaking.

A great palate freshener! Christmas dinner is heavy enough, so this dry and alcoholic iced drink is great either after the main course or after the Christmas pud. (It can be made weeks in advance too.)

There is always a bottle of Scotch around at Christmas and this drink is fantastic for people who aren't quite ready for straight whisky. This drink needs a little pre-thought (you need to flavour some whisky with vanilla beforehand), but it is worth it.

Pomegranita
Serves 8

100 ml/3.5 fl oz gin
juice of 6 pomegranates
1 tbsp caster sugar

Squeeze all the juice and pips from the pomegranates as if they were oranges. The pips contain all that lovely dry juice, so once you have squeezed the juice , pass it through a sieve and crush the pips through the mesh with the back of a tablespoon to extract all the juice from them. Then, in a frost-proof bowl, stir the sugar with the gin and juice until dissolved. Place in the freezer overnight and when you come to serve, just use a fork to break up the block and distribute into small glasses – serve with spoons.

Blizzard
Serves 2

100 ml/3.5 fl oz vanilla-infused whisky (see page 109)
50 ml/1.5 fl oz coconut cream (the thick creamy carton stuff, not the canned)
4 tsp caster sugar
juice of ½ lime
nutmeg

In a cocktail shaker, dissolve the sugar in the lime juice first. Then add the whisky and coconut, shake with cubed ice and strain into ice-filled tumblers. Grate a little nutmeg onto the surface of the drink to finish.

An easy-drinking, tequila-based punch. The secret with this drink is to use both freshly pressed apple juice and freshly squeezed orange juice.

This is a very flexible rum punch – you can use any tropical fruit juice so long as you have a good balance between the sweet and sour elements. The inclusion of sorrel syrup makes this Jamaican punch authentic, but it can be tricky to get hold of, so you can substitute strawberry syrup or grenadine instead. Or just use caster sugar to taste.

Tequila Boom-de-ay

Serves 10

500 ml/16 fl oz tequila
250 ml/8 fl oz crème de cassis
500 ml/16 fl oz orange juice
500 ml/16 fl oz cranberry juice
500 ml/16 fl oz apple juice
juice of 5 limes
1 chopped lime for the bowl

Mix the first six ingredients in a large punch bowl with lots of fresh ice. Throw in some lime chunks to decorate and serve in tall glasses.

Jamaican Bucket Punch

Serves 15–20

1 litre/32 fl oz aged rum
1 litre/32 fl oz pineapple juice
1 litre/32 fl oz orange juice
1 litre/32 fl oz mango or passion fruit juice
juice of 8 limes
300 ml/10 fl oz sorrel syrup
chopped fresh fruit such as pineapple, orange
    and lemon for garnish

Put the first six ingredients in a large bucket with lots of ice and mix well. Throw in the chunks of fruit and serve in glasses or disposable cups.

As the name suggests, this shooter starts with the sharp tang of lemon and ends with a nice sweet finish.

This is a really easy drink to serve at parties because everyone can just DIY bartend (which leaves the hosts free to enjoy themselves!).

Sweet Ending
Serves 10

250 ml/8 fl oz tequila
125 ml/4 fl oz peach schnapps
250 ml/8 fl oz pineapple juice
1 lemon, sliced into 10 pieces

Using lots of ice, shake the hell out of the first three ingredients until icy cold. Strain into the shot glasses and rest a piece of the lemon on the top of each drink. Distribute to your friends and get them to bite into the lemon first, then down the shooter.

Hokey Cokey
Serves 20

2 bottles vodka
20 lemons
5 litres/8 pints freshly pressed apple juice or cranberry juice

Using a potato peeler, remove the peel from the lemons in thin strips and put all the peel into a large punch/washing-up bowl. Then pour over the vodka and leave for at least an hour. Decant the juice into jugs and put some ice to hand in another bowl. When people start arriving, put a ladle or a jug in the homemade lemon vodka, give out plastic cups as they come in and let your guests help themselves as and when they want.

Tip 3 When serving more than one drink from a shaker, pour out a little at a time into each glass. This means that if you are making a round of shots and you've underestimated, then everyone gets a little less and you don't end up with one person who doesn't get any!

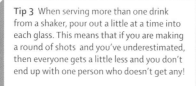

This drink was created in the company of good friends on New Year's Eve, 2003, in Australia. The organized amongst us will prepare the nectarines beforehand by either making a purée or just dicing the nectarines and leaving them in the fridge. (For puréeing hints see 'How To' section, page 110.)

This civilized celebratory drink requires a little preparation – but this can be done in advance. (I am sure your guests will appreciate the effort.) For an extra kick, add a touch of gin to each glass.

Coal Cliff Bellini

Serves 6

150 ml/5 fl oz vodka
3 ripe nectarines, stoned and chopped
juice of 2 lemons
4 tbsp caster sugar
champagne or prosecco

Throw the first four ingredients into a blender with a handful of crushed ice. When everything has been fully blended, pour into tall glasses and top up with fizz.

Pear and Elderflower Fizz

Serves 6

1 ripe pear, peeled and chopped
150 ml/5 fl oz elderflower cordial
1 bottle of champagne/prosecco
6 sprigs of mint for garnish

Throw the chopped pear into a blender with the elderflower cordial and blend until puréed. Then just pour evenly into 6 champagne glasses, top up with fizz and garnish with mint.

Both of these are good fun at parties – make them the day before for best results.

Gin Jelly
Serves 8

150 ml/5 fl oz gin
1 packet of lime jelly (135 g/5 oz)
100 ml/3.5 fl oz boiling water
juice of 1 lime
8 fresh raspberries

Break up the jelly into small pieces and put into a pan with 100 ml (3.5 fl oz) boiling water. Stir over a low heat until the jelly has dissolved. Add the gin and the lime juice, stir well and pour into shot glasses with a raspberry in each glass. Leave in the fridge until set and serve with spoons.

Diablo Jelly
Serves 8

150 ml/5 fl oz tequila
1 packet of blackcurrrant jelly (135 g/5 oz)
100 ml/3.5 fl oz boiling water
juice of 1 lime
8 fresh blackcurrants/blueberries

Follow the same method for Gin Jelly, but use blackcurrant jelly and tequila instead of lime and gin, and garnish either with blackcurrants or blackberries.

With this large cosmopolitan cocktail you'll be able to watch the whole of the *Sex and the City* series back to back without getting up (or without getting your partner to make it).

Rent a movie, put your feet up and drink this all night. It is easy to make and even easier to drink.

Pint of Cosmo

Serves 1 lush

100 ml/3.5 fl oz vodka (citrus-flavoured is best)
50 ml/1.5 fl oz orange liqueur
2 tbsp caster sugar
juice of 1 lime
juice of ½ lemon
15 ml/1 tbsp lime cordial
200 ml/7 fl oz cranberry juice
1 strip of orange peel

In a cocktail shaker, dissolve the caster sugar in the citrus juice first, then chuck in the vodka and other liquids and shake with lots of ice. Strain into a large, ice-filled pint glass and use the orange peel to zest the oil from the skin over the surface of the drink.

Blockbuster

Serves 1

50 ml/1.5 fl oz aged rum
200 ml/7 fl oz cola
200 ml/7 fl oz ginger beer
juice of 1 lime

Pour all the ingredients into a large glass filled with ice and stir.

Tip 4 When squeezing lemons and limes that are not fully ripe, roll them between your hand and a hard surface with as much pressure as you can. This loosens the juice making them easier to squeeze.

Delicate, sweet and sophisticated – hard not to love!

A spectacular hot concoction. Don't leave the drinks burning too long as the glasses will get very hot! As you drink, the chocolate melts and by the time you get to the bottom of the glass, it is totally gooey and delicious. If this after-dinner, Black Forest Gâteau night-cap doesn't get you in the mood, then nothing will.

Love Soane
Serves 2

25 ml/1 fl oz gin
juice of 1 lime
50 ml/1.5 fl oz passion fruit juice
2 tsp caster sugar
champagne
2 strips of lemon peel

In a cocktail shaker, dissolve the sugar in the lime juice first. Then add the gin and the passion fruit juice and shake with cubed ice. Strain evenly into two champagne glasses and top up with champagne. Zest the surface of each drink with the strips of lemon peel.

Light My Fire
Serves 2

75 ml/2.5 fl oz brandy
25 ml/1 fl oz cherry liqueur
2 chocolate truffles

Buy two of the richest, most expensive handmade chocolates that you can (try and buy the ones that don't have any cocoa powder on the outside) and put them in the bottom of two shot glasses. Then, in a saucepan, gently heat the brandy and cherry liqueur until warmed through (not too hot to drink, though). Pour the mixture over the chocolates and light the brandy. Turn the lights down (maybe they are already down) and serve them flaming.

A delicious, fun, Hallowe'en party drink. The sparkly effect of the burning cinnamon gives a lovely cinnamon-toast smell to the room and makes the drink taste great.

A rich blood-coloured cocktail. Very dry and drinkable (and much more tasty than real blood).

Voodoo

Serves 2

100 ml/3.5 fl oz aged rum
50 ml/1.5 fl oz sweet vermouth
1 ½ tbsp caster sugar
200ml/7 fl oz apple juice
juice of 1 lime
ground cinnamon

In a cocktail shaker, dissolve the sugar in the lime juice first. Then shake the rest of the ingredients (except the cinnamon) with cubed ice and strain into the ice filled highballs. Dim the lights and hold a lit match or lighter above the surface of the drink. Sprinkle some ground cinnamon over the flame and watch the spice sparkle as it burns.

Bloody Breeze

Serves 1

25 ml/1 fl oz aged rum
25 ml/1 fl oz crème de cassis
75 ml/2.5 fl oz cranberry juice
75 ml/2.5 fl oz pink grapefruit juice
1 wedge of lime

Fill a highball glass with ice and pour in the first four ingredients. Squeeze a wedge of lime into the drink and drop it in.

Booze with food

In many cases, a cocktail will act as an aperitif to stimulate the appetite and prepare the stomach for the food that follows. In this chapter, I have included some traditional aperitifs, some drinks to complement food while eating, shots to refresh the palate after eating and drinks that are rich and sweet like desserts.

Indian

I have to admit that an ice-cold beer is hard to substitute when choosing a drink to accompany an Indian curry. However, this fortified lassi is deliciously cooling with a vindaloo or a jalfrezi and can also be made without alcohol (use one-third less sugar).

A perfect way to end an Indian meal – sharp, strong and refreshing on the palate.

Be-a-Substitute

Serves 2

100 ml/3.5 fl oz vodka
pinch of saffron threads plus extra for garnish
3 tbsp caster sugar
3 tbsp Greek yoghurt
200 ml/7 fl oz coconut milk
juice of 2 limes
pinch of ground cardamom

Put the saffron in a cocktail shaker with the vodka. Stir the saffron in the vodka for a few seconds or until the vodka turns yellow, then stir in the sugar until dissolved. Add the remaining ingredients, shake with cubed ice and strain into ice-filled beer mugs or highball glasses. Garnish with a few saffron threads for colour.

Colonial Conclusion

Serves 4

100 ml/3.5 fl oz gin
3 tbsp mango sorbet
juice of 1 lemon

Put all the ingredients into a shaker with ice, shake hard and strain into shot glasses.

A great after-dinner cocktail – cooling and tangy after spicy food, but as sweet and smooth as a dessert.

An exotic take on the classic strawberry-and-champagne mix. The rose water just adds to the delicate taste of the champagne and gives it a little bitterness.

Monday in Marrakech
Serves 2

100 ml/3.5 fl oz vodka
juice of 1 lemon
4 tsp caster sugar
2 scoops vanilla ice cream
pinch ground cinnamon

Blend the first four ingredients with a handful of crushed ice and, when smooth, serve in champagne flutes. Dust with cinnamon.

Persian Prince
Serves 1

25 ml/1 fl oz vodka
25ml/1 fl oz strawberry coulis/purée
1 tsp rose water
champagne
slice of strawberry or a rose petal for garnish
    (optional)

Either buy the coulis or just blend some strawberries (see 'How to' page 110) and spoon the purée into the bottom of a champagne glass. Then add the vodka and the rosewater and top up with champagne. Stir well and garnish with a slice of strawberry or a rose petal if you like.

It is amazing how the harshness of tequila is tamed in this drink by the sweet-sour flavour of the clementine. This is a great little drink any time of the day and can be used as a hangover cure in extreme cases.

This has a light and delicate fruitiness which acts as an alcoholic starter to get the gastric juices flowing.

Mexican Breakfast

Serves 1

50 ml/1.5 fl oz tequila
1 whole clementine, quartered (skin 'n' all)
1 tsp caster sugar (or to taste)

Using the blunt end of a rolling pin or a pestle, crush the clementine with the sugar in a cocktail shaker until the sugar has dissolved and all the juice from the clementine has been extracted. Add the tequila and some crushed ice and shake hard. Strain into a martini glass.

Señorita

Serves 2

100 ml/3.5 fl oz tequila
100 ml/3.5 fl oz pink grapefruit juice
½ honeydew melon, peeled, seeded and sliced
1 tbsp caster sugar

There are two ways to make this drink. Either just chuck everything in a blender with crushed ice and blend until smooth, or blend the melon with the sugar first and then shake the resulting purée with the grapefruit juice and tequila and strain over ice.

This drink was created by bartending legend Dick Bradsell. It is such a great little after-dinner cocktail that I had to include it in the book, but it only really works if you can make espresso at home. If you can't, then get a local bartender to mix it up for you.

This is my twist on the classic daiquiri. It is quite a tangy drink, but laced with richness from the brandy and sweetness from the vanilla sugar.

Vodka Espresso

Serves 2

100 ml/3.5 fl oz vodka
1 double espresso
3 tsp caster sugar (or to taste)
coffee beans for garnish

Firstly, make the espresso and dissolve in the sugar. Fill a cocktail shaker with ice, then add the sweetened coffee and the vodka and shake hard. Strain into small glasses filled with ice or into martini glasses. Garnish with one, three or five coffee beans (an odd number for luck).

French Daiquiri

Serves 2

100 ml/3.5 fl oz brandy
2 tbsp vanilla sugar (see page 114)
juice of 1½ limes

In a cocktail shaker, stir together the sugar with the lime juice until the sugar is dissolved, then add the brandy and cubed ice and shake hard. Strain into martini glasses.

This is how to impress your guests and be the host with the most. The grapefruit and champagne make a great flavour combination. It is a slightly tart but very refreshing drink that can be made well in advance.

Don't be put off by the egg. It gives the drink a really nice rich creamy texture – although be careful with raw eggs! Make sure they are super-fresh. The nutmeg is really important as it sets off the brandy and the nuttiness of the amaretto. Perfect for after dinner.

Champagne & Pink Grapefruit Granita

Serves 6

250 ml/8 fl oz champagne
50 ml/1.5 fl oz vodka
juice of 1 pink grapefruit
2 tbsp caster sugar

Pour the grapefruit juice and any pulp into a frost-proof bowl. Stir in the sugar until dissolved and add the champagne and vodka. Place the bowl in the freezer for at least six hours or overnight until frozen. Then either break it up with a fork or whizz it in a blender for a second to break it up a little. Pour into small glasses and serve with teaspoons.

St Germain

Serves 2

50 ml/1.5 fl oz brandy
25 ml/1 fl oz amaretto
1 tbsp caster sugar
50 ml/1.5 fl oz single cream
50 ml/1.5 fl oz milk
1 egg yolk
whole nutmeg

In a cocktail shaker, stir together the sugar and the brandy first until the sugar is dissolved, then shake everything except the nutmeg hard with cubed ice and strain into martini glasses. Grate a little fresh nutmeg on the top of each drink to finish.

This drink is based on Campari, which I now love, but used to hate. It is one of those spirits that your uncle brings back from his package holiday and the thing sits ominously in your parents' drinks cabinet for years doing nothing. They say that it takes at least five attempts at trying Campari before you start to acquire the taste – here is number one.

The peach gives the wine a very subtle, fresh fragrance. It is an ideal partner for drawn-out Italian feasts in the garden. In the south of Italy they have been doing this for years, and it was the inspiration for Giuseppe Cipriani's Bellini cocktail which was invented in 1948 in Venice using white peach purée and prosecco.

Ignorance is Bliss

Serves 2

50 ml/1.5 fl oz Campari
50 ml/1.5 fl oz vodka (citrus works best)
2 tsp caster sugar
50 ml/1.5 fl oz apple juice
50 ml/1.5 fl oz passion fruit juice
2 lime wedges

In a cocktail shaker, dissolve the sugar in the vodka first. Then add the Campari and fruit juices and shake hard with cubed ice. Strain into martini glasses, squeeze a wedge of lime into each drink and then drop it in.

Bellini Wine

Serves 1–4

1 bottle dry white Italian wine
3 ripe peaches

Simply cut the peaches in half (leaving the stones in) and leave them in a jug with the wine in the fridge for a couple of days. Once you have enjoyed the wine, you can then eat the peaches as dessert with some double cream. Delicious!

This may sound like an odd concoction, but cucumber is fantastic in cocktails. This drink is fresh, crisp and very moreish.

The gin combined with the fresh basil and grapes makes a very aromatic and delicate flavoured cocktail. It is light and refreshing and works well as an aperitif to Greek salads and dips.

Two Inches of Cucumber

Serves 2

100 ml/3.5 fl oz vodka
25 ml/1 fl oz orange liqueur
2 inches of cucumber, peeled and chopped
juice of ½ lemon
1 tbsp caster sugar
2 strips of lemon peel

If you have a blender or a food processor, blend the first five ingredients with a handful of ice until slushy and serve. If you don't, then use the end of a rolling pin or a wooden pestle to crush the cucumber in the bottom of a cocktail shaker with the sugar and lemon juice. Add the vodka and orange liqueur and ice and shake well. Strain into martini glasses and zest the top of each drink with the lemon peel.

Mediterranean Martini

Serves 2

100 ml/3.5 fl oz gin
15 tasty white grapes
2 tbsp caster sugar
15 fresh basil leaves (+2 for garnish)
juice of 1 lemon

Crush the grapes, sugar and basil leaves in the bottom of a cocktail shaker using the end of a rolling pin or a wooden pestle. When all the juice has been squashed out of the grapes, add the gin and lemon juice and shake with cubed ice. Strain into martini glasses and garnish with a basil leaf.

Tip 5 When using caster sugar, always dissolve it in any citrus juice first as the acid helps break down the sugar. If there is no citrus in the drink, dissolve the sugar in room-temperature alcohol first.

The tequila gives this drink a lightly aromatic quality, the mint gives fragrance and the guava makes it exotic – a delicious combo!

There are whole books written on this classic cocktail. All I am going to say about it is, once you start drinking martinis, you will never turn back. You can, of course, make martinis with vodka, too. The purity of the neat spirit complements the simplicity of the flavours of Japanese food really well.

Lotus Flower

Serves 2

100 ml/3.5 fl oz tequila
12 mint leaves (+2 sprigs for garnish)
400 ml/14 fl oz guava juice

Rip the mint leaves into a cocktail shaker, then add the tequila and the guava juice and shake everything hard with cubed ice. Strain into ice-filled highball glasses and garnish each one with a sprig of mint.

For convenience, I always keep both my gin and vodka in the freezer and just pour the thick and oily frozen spirit into a frozen glass with a splash of cold vermouth. Liquid heaven!

Dry Martini (classic)

Serves 2

200 ml/7 fl oz gin
1 tbsp dry vermouth
2 strips of lemon peel or 2 green olives

This is the classic way to make a Martini. Have your glasses ready chilled and garnish each drink either with a green olive (one that has been preserved in brine, not oil) or a strip of lemon peel. Fill a cocktail shaker to the brim with ice. Pour a splash of vermouth over the ice and stir briefly. Now strain off any excess vermouth (this coats the ice with vermouth), pour in the gin and stir around 20 times or until ice-cold. Strain into chilled martini glasses. Then either zest the oil from the lemon peel over the glass or garnish each drink with a single olive – the choice is yours.

This drink is tangy, refreshing, and has loads of flavour. It gets the juices flowing before a take-away, or cuts through the MSG afterwards.

This is a delicate, subtle and dry drink. It complements all curries well, but is really refreshing with a fiery green or red Thai curry.

Easy Tiger
Serves 4

200 ml/7 fl oz tequila
50 ml/1.5 fl oz clear honey
juice of 4 limes
1 tsp freshly grated ginger (or 1 tbsp ginger cordial)
orange peel for garnish

Stir the honey with the lime juice and tequila so that it dissolves. Then add the ginger and shake with cubed ice. Strain into four champagne flutes. Garnish each drink with a long strip of orange peel twisted around the inside of the glass.

Jasmine Punch
Serves 4

200 ml/7 fl oz gin
50 ml/1.5 fl oz peach schnapps
2 lemons
4 jasmine tea bags (or 6 tsp loose tea)
450 ml/15 fl oz boiling water
200 ml/7 fl oz apple juice
2 tbsp caster sugar

Before squeezing the lemons, cut four strips of peel from one of them. Then, in a large heatproof serving bowl, steep the tea in the boiling water for a minute. Strain the tea and stir in the sugar and remaining ingredients. Fill the bowl with ice cubes to chill it down and, when ready, serve the punch in highball glasses filled with ice. Zest the lemon peel over the surface of each drink.

The word 'punch' comes from the Hindi for five, *panch*, and refers to the ingredients: spirit, tea, lemon juice, sugar and water that were adopted when Britain colonized India in the 1600s.

Tangy and tropical, the ginger and the mango taste great together.

This may seem an odd mix of flavours, but the delicacy of the guava complements the complexity of the malt perfectly – try it!

Mango No. 5
Serves 3

75 ml/2.5 fl oz vodka
25 ml/1 fl oz orange liqueur
2 tsp caster sugar
juice of 1 lime
300 ml/10 fl oz mango juice
½ tsp freshly grated ginger (or 2 tsp ginger cordial)

In a cocktail shaker, dissolve the sugar in the lime juice to start with and then shake the remaining ingredients with cubed ice and strain into martini glasses.

Unlikely Marriage
Serves 2

75 ml/2.5 fl oz whisky
25 ml/ 1 fl oz orange liqueur
juice of 1 lemon
300 ml/10 fl oz guava juice
2 wedges of lemon for garnish (optional)

Shake the first four ingredients with cubed ice and strain into ice-filled highballs. If you wish, garnish each glass with a small wedge of lemon.

An easy and delicious variation on the classic, colonial invention.

This is my own take on the classic Gimlet. The marmalade makes this a wonderfully tangy and moreish pre-dinner cocktail.

GE&T
Serves 1

50 ml/1.5 fl oz gin
25 ml/1 fl oz elderflower cordial
200 ml/7 fl oz tonic water
1 large lemon wedge

Pour the ingredients into an ice-filled highball glass and stir. Squeeze the lemon juice into the drink and serve.

The Limey
Serves 2

100 ml/3.5 fl oz gin
2 tbsp caster sugar
2 tsp lime marmalade
juice of 2 limes

In a cocktail shaker, stir the caster sugar with the lime juice until it is dissolved, then add the other ingredients and shake hard – until your hands hurt from the cold. Strain into chilled martini glasses using a sieve to remove lime peel and tiny bits of ice.

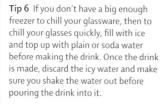

Tip 6 If you don't have a big enough freezer to chill your glassware, then to chill your glasses quickly, fill with ice and top up with plain or soda water before making the drink. Once the drink is made, discard the icy water and make sure you shake the water out before pouring the drink into it.

The mixture of lemon, lime and orange works well with the beer and creates a long and refreshing alternative to straight beer.

Not the healthiest way to start the day. Try this as a cure from the hangover from hell… or just enjoy it as a flavour-packed, all-day cocktail.

Dandy Shandy

Serves 1

25 ml/1 fl oz orange liqueur
150 ml/5 fl oz chilled lager
150 ml/5 fl oz lemonade
½ lime, cut into wedges

Pour the first three ingredients into a large glass and squeeze the lime wedges into the drink, dropping them in afterwards.

American Breakfast

Serves 2

50 ml/1.5 fl oz bourbon
juice from 4 freshly squeezed pink grapefruits
(or 200 ml/7 fl oz carton grapefruit juice)

25 ml/1 fl oz maple syrup

Fill a cocktail shaker with cubed ice, pour in all the ingredients and shake hard. Serve tall over cubed ice.

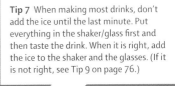

Tip 7 When making most drinks, don't add the ice until the last minute. Put everything in the shaker/glass first and then taste the drink. When it is right, add the ice to the shaker and the glasses. (If it is not right, see Tip 9 on page 76.)

Out & about

This is the shortest chapter because, like sex, we do it at home more than out in the open.

Here are some good ideas to stimulate you when you are playing away from home.

This is my version of a mulled wine/vin chaud/ glüwein and is great for all kinds of events such as camping outdoors, or even sailing or skiing.

This drink is light, dry, fruity and easily quaffable.

Carry On Camping

Serves 2–4

1 bottle full-bodied red wine (a rich, New World version
  of Cabernet Sauvignon is good)
12 whole cloves
1 stick of cinnamon
2 slices of fresh root ginger
pinch ground nutmeg
2 tbsp caster sugar
juice of ½ lemon

Take a swig out of the bottle of wine, then stuff all the spices, the sugar and the lemon juice into the bottle and re-cork. The bottle is best left at least 12 hours or even a couple of weeks, although it is fine drunk straight away. When you are on-site, decant the contents of the bottle into a pan and heat it up gently on a camping stove; drink warm in heatproof cups.

Blood, Sweat & Sand

Serves 2–4 (Makes 1 litre)

100 ml/3.5 fl oz brandy
50 ml/1.5 fl oz crème de cassis
juice of 1½ limes
800 ml/26 fl oz chilled cranberry juice

Pour all the ingredients into a chilled thermos (vacuum) flask. If you have a large thermos, you can always add a handful of ice cubes for extra chilling.

This is a very easy, refreshing drink to make. If you like more of a kick to it, then add gin or vodka.

As Lou Reed suggests, this sangria is perfect for drinking in the park.

Park Life

Serves 4

200 ml/7 fl oz Pimm's No. 1 Cup
½ chilled cucumber, peeled
1 litre/32 fl oz chilled white grape juice
   or apple juice

Chop up the cucumber into smallish, crudité-sized batons and throw them into a large, chilled thermos (vacuum) flask. Add the Pimm's and the fruit juice – plus some ice, if you want – and off you go!

Grassyarse Señor

Serves 2–4

1 bottle Spanish red wine (Rioja works well)
splash of brandy
splash of orange liqueur
1 orange
1 lime
1 tbsp caster sugar

Open the wine and start drinking a glass. While you are enjoying the wine, cut the orange and the lime in half and squeeze out the juice from one half of each. Then cut the other halves into small pieces and stuff them, the squeezed juice and a splash each of brandy and orange liqueur into the bottle until it is full. Re-cork the bottle. If you are the kind of person to plan things in advance, then stick it in the fridge for a couple of hours to chill, otherwise pack a picnic, some plastic glasses and a rug and off you go.

This a simple but effective whisky drink. The flavour of fresh vanilla exaggerates the vanilla aroma present in the Scotch (which comes from the wooden barrels in which it is aged), while the sugar gives it a mellow finish.

A rich, smooth, sexy, old-fashioned style of hot chocolate – with a kick. You can use any of the spirits listed below, the choice is yours. Do make sure you buy good-quality chocolate containing at least 75 per cent cocoa solids, and, ideally, use full-fat milk.

Vanilla Hot Scotch

Serves 4

300 ml/10 fl oz whisky
½ vanilla pod, diced
2 tsp soft brown sugar

You can make this in one of two ways. Either chuck all the ingredients into a bottle and then decant and heat it up on location, or heat the mixture up in a small pan over medium heat before going out, then pour it into a preheated thermos (vacuum) flask. Either way, heat all the ingredients together gently until warm. To serve, strain through a sieve into heatproof glasses, discarding the bits of vanilla pod.

Hot-digidy-Chocolate

Serves 4

200 ml/7 fl oz brandy/rum/whisky/bourbon
250 ml/8 fl oz milk
250 ml/8 fl oz water
100 g dark chocolate
3 tbsp caster sugar

Heat the milk and the water in a pan until almost boiling. Break up the chocolate into small bits and slowly stir into the hot milk over a medium-low heat. When all the chocolate is melted and the mix is smooth, stir in the sugar until dissolved and slug in the spirit of choice. When it is piping hot, transfer it to a pre-heated thermos (vacuum) flask or a hip flask and drink shortly afterwards.

You can serve this drink hot, cold or this way, at room temperature. I personally find that the flavours of the brandy with the ginger are great served at room temperature. You can make this with Stones ginger wine, although fresh ginger tastes much better and gives more of a spicy kick.

An easy drinkin', easy sippin' train drink.

Ginger Snap
Serves 4

200 ml/7 fl oz brandy
8 slices of fresh root ginger
1 tbsp caster sugar

Using the end of a rolling pin or a wooden pestle, bash the ginger and sugar together in the bottom of a cocktail shaker. When the sugar has dissolved in the ginger juice, add the brandy, stir together well and sieve before decanting into an empty bottle or a hip flask.

Tennessee Travel Companion
Serves 2–4

200 ml/7 fl oz bourbon
4 tsp maple syrup
juice of 2 lemons
600 ml/20 fl oz chilled apple juice

Mix all the ingredients with some ice in a large jug and stir thoroughly to chill down further. Transfer to a pre-chilled thermos (vacuum) flask and it's ready to go.

Here's a variation which serves 8
To flavour a whole bottle of brandy, use 15 thick slices of ginger and 4 tablespoons of caster sugar and just leave the flavourings in the brandy for a couple of days to infuse in the bottle.

Wonderfully aromatic and full of juicy, warming flavours. This certainly hits the spot if you are feeling chilled to the bone.

Tea is very refreshing and this (not over-potent) cold, bourbon-based cocktail is great for lazy summer beach days. Remember to chill the thermos (vacuum) flask before you head for the sun (see page 116 for details).

French Toddy

Serves 2

100 ml/3.5 fl oz brandy
50 ml/1.5 fl oz crème de cassis
12 whole cloves

There are two ways to do this. Either chuck all the ingredients into a bottle and heat on location, or heat in a small pan over medium heat before going out, then pour it into a pre-heated thermos (vacuum) flask. Either way, heat all the ingredients together gently and, when ready to serve, pour into heatproof glasses, leaving the cloves in if you like.

Bourbon Beach Iced Tea

Serves 4–6 (Makes 1.5 litres/48 fl oz)

150 ml/5 fl oz bourbon
2 tea bags
800 ml/26 fl oz boiling water
175 ml/7 fl oz caster sugar
juice of 4 lemons
500 ml/16 fl oz cold water

Steep the tea bags in a heatproof glass or ceramic bowl in the boiling water for no more than a minute. Remove the tea bags and stir in the sugar. When the sugar has dissolved, add the remaining ingredients and leave in the fridge to chill right down (overnight is best). Transfer to a chilled thermos (vacuum) flask – and don't forget your factor 15!

Winter warmers

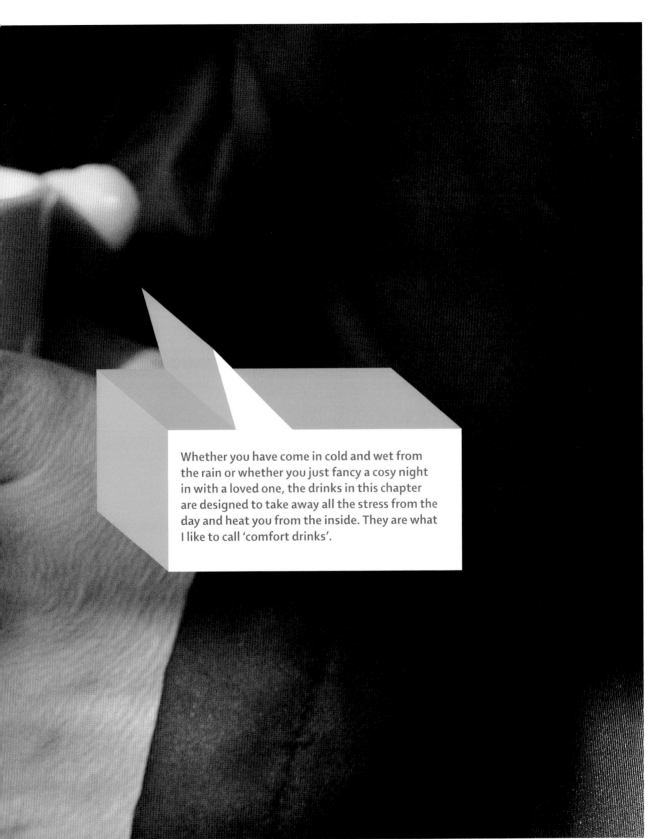

Whether you have come in cold and wet from the rain or whether you just fancy a cosy night in with a loved one, the drinks in this chapter are designed to take away all the stress from the day and heat you from the inside. They are what I like to call 'comfort drinks'.

Not as alcoholic as some of the drinks in this chapter, but just as warming and comforting. The brave add a pinch of dried chilli flakes to the mix.

An Irish coffee is a fantastic way to end a meal, although making it yourself can be a nightmare if you don't know the details. The trick with making this drink is preparation. (It doesn't make much difference if you use Irish, Scottish, or even Japanese whisky in this drink as long as it is not a single malt.)

Hot Spiced Cider

Serves 4

1 litre/32 fl oz medium sweet cider
4 tbsp maple syrup or honey
skin of 1 orange
2 cinnamon sticks
small handful of whole cloves
2 tsp ground allspice

Put all the ingredients into a saucepan, heat gently and stir occasionally for around 15 minutes (do not boil). When hot, strain into heatproof cups (leaving the flavourings in if you want) and enjoy.

Irish Coffee (classic)

Serves 1

25ml /1 fl oz whisky
50 ml/1.5 fl oz whipping cream
200 ml/7 fl oz strong filter/cafetière coffee
2 tsp caster sugar

Preheat a strong wine glass by leaving it in hot water while you prepare the cream. Using a whisk, beat the cream in a bowl until it starts to thicken. Then make your coffee, making sure that it is piping hot. Take the glass out of the hot water and dry it. Add the coffee, sugar and whisky to the glass and stir. Slowly pour the whipped cream over the back of a spoon so that the cream runs onto the top of the coffee.

A great drink to make when you come in late and half frozen – it will thaw you out and will send you to sleep like a baby!

This is perfect home-comfort, evening snooze-booze.

Hot Bourbon with Marmalade

Serves 2

200 ml/7 fl oz bourbon
2 tsp quality orange marmalade
2 tsp soft brown sugar
2 strips of lemon peel

In a saucepan, heat together the first three ingredients until the marmalade has melted and the bourbon is steaming. Strain into heatproof glasses, then zest the oil from the lemon over the surface of the drinks.

Big Baby Milk

Serves 2

50 ml/1.5 fl oz brandy
2 mugs or glasses of milk
freshly grated nutmeg
4 tsp maple syrup

In a saucepan, heat all the ingredients together until warm and serve. Start to feel your eyes slowly getting heavier and hea....

> **Tip 8 Quality control:** You should taste the cocktails before serving to guests so that you know they are getting a good drink. Take a straw, dip it into the drink and place your forefinger over one end. Keep your finger over the end while removing the straw and it will retain a little of the cocktail. Place the end in your mouth and take your finger off. If it doesn't taste right then see Tip 9 on page 76.

This is what I make for myself if I am feeling under the weather, although please don't overdose on flu medicine with alcohol – I don't want to be sued!

This is one of my all-time favourite drinks and one which I couldn't possibly leave out of a cocktail book. It takes a good few minutes to make this drink – but it is worth it.

 or

AK Cold Relief

Serves 1 poorly person

25 ml/1 fl oz brandy or whisky
1 sachet lemon-flavoured cold relief powder
2 tsp honey
juice of ½ lemon

In a mug or heatproof glass, dissolve the lemon powder with the honey and lemon juice in boiling water, add the brandy or whisky and retire to bed.

Old Fashioned (classic)

Serves 1

50 ml/1.5 fl oz bourbon
1 tsp caster sugar
2 dashes Angostura bitters
strip of orange peel for garnish

Take a good-quality tumbler and add the sugar and the bitters. Put just a splash of the bourbon into the glass and start stirring. Keep stirring, adding one cube of ice at a time, gradually filling up the glass with ice cubes (you'll need around five). Add the bourbon and stir until all the sugar has dissolved and the drink is icy cold. Zest the oil from the orange over the surface of the drink.

Although this drink is cold, the flavours of the Scotch with the cherry brandy and passion fruit juice make it an easy drinking, rich and fruity cocktail. Use more passion juice if you want a longer, more refreshing drink.

This drink is deliciously warming with loads of depth and subtle sophistication.

Scottish Sweetheart

Serves 1

50 ml/1.5 fl oz whisky
15 ml/1 tbsp cherry liqueur
100 ml/3.5 fl oz passion fruit juice
1 lemon wedge

Put the first three ingredients into a tumbler filled with cubed ice and stir together. Squeeze the juice from the lemon wedge into the drink and drop it in.

Two's a Pear

Serves 2

100 ml/3.5 fl oz brandy
2 tsp soft brown sugar
2 slices of ripe pear

In a saucepan, slowly heat the brandy with the sugar and slices of pear. After two minutes or so, when the brandy is steaming, remove from the heat and pour the brandy and the pear into two brandy glasses or tumblers.

This classic, sweet, simple drink is ideal as an after-dinner digestif. It's the perfect companion when you're sitting by an open fire listening to the Rat Pack.

This slightly bitter but full-flavoured drink really puts you in the mood for kicking your feet through piles of crisp brown leaves (watch out for those hedgehogs though). Don't be put off by the balsamic – this is a cocktail of depth, mystery and intrigue.

Godfather (classic)

Serves 1 Don

25ml/1 fl oz whisky
25ml/1 fl oz amaretto

In a tumbler, mix the whisky and amaretto with large chunks of ice. Stir well and drink at leisure.

Autumn Martini

Serves 2

100 ml/3.5 fl oz port
100 ml/3.5 fl oz cranberry juice
15 raspberries (+2 for garnish)
1 tsp balsamic vinegar

Put all the ingredients except the garnish into a cocktail shaker with cubed ice and shake vigorously until the raspberries have been crushed. Strain through a sieve into martini glasses (to remove all the raspberry bits) and garnish each drink with a raspberry.

A rich and complex bourbon drink with a nice little kick coming from the chilli.

The honey and orange are a simple but perfect mix of flavours. Very warming and soothing.

Spicy Mash
Serves 1

50 ml/1.5 fl oz bourbon
⅓ orange, chopped into wedges
1 tsp honey
thin slice of red chilli

Using the end of a rolling pin or a wooden pestle crush the orange, the honey and the chilli in the bottom of a chunky tumbler until all the juice has been extracted from the orange and the honey has dissolved. Fill the glass with crushed ice and pour in the bourbon. Stir well.

Hot Rum & Orange
Serves 4

300 ml/10 fl oz aged rum
peel of 1 orange
1 tbsp honey or soft brown sugar

Put the orange peel in a saucepan with the rum and honey or sugar and heat together gently. When warmed through (do not boil), strain into heatproof glasses.

Steamy summers

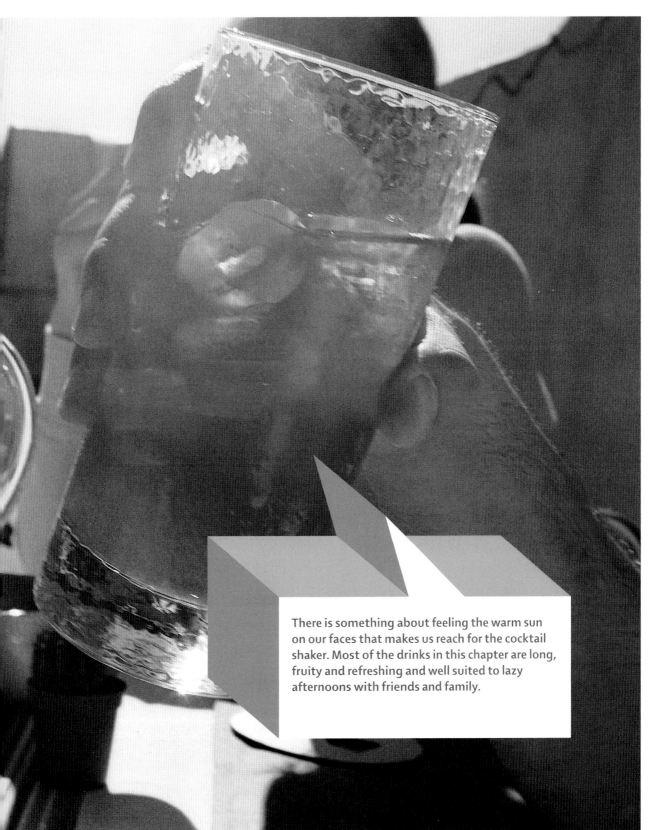

There is something about feeling the warm sun on our faces that makes us reach for the cocktail shaker. Most of the drinks in this chapter are long, fruity and refreshing and well suited to lazy afternoons with friends and family.

Cool, dry and summery. Be careful not to get this on your tennis shorts – it will stain.

A deliciously tangy, smooth drink. The ginger complements the peach beautifully.

Anyone For Tennis?
Serves 1 player

50 ml/1.5 fl oz port
4 strawberries, chopped (+1 for garnish)
juice of ½ lemon
2 tsp caster sugar
50 ml/1.5 fl oz cranberry juice

Using the end of a rolling pin or a wooden pestle, crush the strawberries with the lemon juice and sugar in the bottom of a tumbler. Then fill the glass with crushed ice, add the port and cranberry juice and stir well. Garnish with a sliced strawberry.

Kiss My Peach
Serves 2

100 ml/3.5 fl oz vodka
1 ripe peach, stoned and sliced
½ tsp freshly grated root ginger or 10 ml/2 tsp
   ginger cordial
juice of 1 lime
5 tsp caster sugar

Blend all the ingredients with crushed ice until smooth. Pour into champagne glasses or martini glasses to serve.

This is a more interesting variant on the classic Tom Collins and makes a tasty long drink.

The fresh basil in this drink brings out the complexity of the gin and the freshness of the raspberries – a delicious drink!

Blackberry Collins
Serves 4

200 ml/7 fl oz gin
30 plump, juicy blackberries
juice of 2 lemons
4 tbsp caster sugar
approx. 400 ml/14 fl oz soda water

Mush up the blackberries, lemon juice and sugar in a cocktail shaker using the end of a rolling pin or a wooden pestle, then add the gin and ice and shake hard until cold. Pour evenly into 4 highball glasses filled with cubed ice and top up with soda water.

Ruby Tuesday
Serves 2

100 ml/3.5 fl oz gin
2 tsp caster sugar
juice of 1 lime
15 raspberries (+2 for garnish)
10 basil leaves (+2 for garnish)
75 ml/2.5 fl oz apple juice

In a cocktail shaker, stir the sugar with the lime juice until dissolved. Then add the gin, raspberries, basil and apple juice and shake hard with cubed ice. Strain through a sieve into martini glasses. Make a boat from a basil leaf and a passenger from a raspberry to garnish each drink.

Tip 9 Sometimes, a drink it just doesn't quite taste right, it can be a little bland or too strong. (If it is too sweet, it will be obvious.) I often find that drinks at this stage need more sugar to carry through the flavours. Just add a little at a time until it tastes right.

Easy to make, deeply tropical and tangy.

This drink's name refers to the origins of the word 'posh' which described those high-class travellers who went by sea to India and back in colonial times and who could afford the more expensive, shady side of the boat – 'port out, starboard home'. The word 'punch' also originates from India – as does the use of tonic water.

Totally Tropical

Serves 1

50 ml/1.5 fl oz aged rum
25 ml/1 fl oz orange liqueur
150 ml/5 fl oz mango juice
juice of ½ lemon

Fill a highball glass with cubed ice, pour in all the ingredients and stir well.

POSH Punch

Serves 1

50 ml/1.5 fl oz port
1 tbsp caster sugar
juice of ½ lime
75 ml/2.5 fl oz apple juice
50 ml/1.5 fl oz tonic water
slice of apple or a strawberry for garnish

In the bottom of a highball glass, dissolve the sugar in the lime juice first. Then add the port, apple juice and cubed ice and top up with tonic water. Garnish with a slice of apple or a strawberry.

The idea for this drink came from the Brazilian Caipirinha. It is tangy and refreshing and leaves a good puckering in your mouth.

This is an easy-drinking cocktail with a citrusy tang of lime and lemon. The subtleties of the ginger ale work well with the aged rum.

St Clement's Crush

Serves 2

100 ml/3.5 fl oz gin
1 lemon, cut into eight wedges
1 orange, cut into eight wedges
2 tbsp caster sugar

Using a rolling pin or a wooden pestle, crush the citrus wedges and sugar together in the bottom of a cocktail shaker until all their juices have been extracted and the sugar is dissolved. Add the gin, fill the shaker with crushed ice and shake hard and fast. Pour everything evenly into highball glasses.

Jamaica?

Serves 1

50 ml/1.5 fl oz aged rum
juice of ½ lemon
juice of ½ lime
1 tbsp caster sugar
1 tsp lime cordial
150 ml/5 fl oz ginger ale
slice of lime for garnish (optional)

In the bottom of a highball glass, dissolve the sugar in the citrus juices. Then fill the glass with ice and pour in the rum and lime cordial. Top up with ginger ale and garnish with a slice of lime.

A kiwi fruit has nine times more vitamin C than an orange, which means that even though there is a slug of brandy in this drink, it must be good for you! You can use vodka, rum or tequila as alternatives to brandy.

The grapefruit gives a pleasant bitterness to the fresh raspberries and makes a lovely, fresh, summery drink.

The Kiwi
Serves 1

50 ml/1.5 fl oz brandy
1 kiwi fruit, peeled and cut into 6 pieces
juice of ½ lemon
3 tsp soft brown sugar

Using the end of a rolling pin or a wooden pestle, crush the kiwi with the sugar in the bottom of a tumbler. Then add the brandy and the lemon juice and fill the glass with crushed ice.

Summer Breeze
Serves 2

100 ml/3.5 fl oz vodka
200 ml/7 fl oz grapefruit juice
20 raspberries (+2 for garnish)
4 tsp caster sugar

Put all the ingredients into a cocktail shaker with loads of ice and shake hard until the raspberries have been mashed up. Then strain into short glasses filled with cubed ice. Garnish each glass with a fresh raspberry.

This is a great drink if you are partial to the odd whisky, but fancy something longer and more refreshing.

The good thing about this drink is that you can make it for anyone's tastes. Use lemonade to make it sweeter, use tonic to make it bitter, use the champagne to make it drier or the soda to make it more refreshing and light.

Summer in Speyside

Serves 2

50 ml/1.5 fl oz whisky
50 ml/1.5 fl oz orange liqueur
2 tsp caster sugar
juice of 1 lime
200 ml/7 fl oz apple juice

In the bottom of a cocktail shaker dissolve the sugar with the lime juice. Add the remaining ingredients and some ice cubes and shake well. Strain into ice-filled tumblers.

Blueberry Sling

Serves 2

50 ml/1.5 fl oz tequila
25 ml/1 fl oz crème de cassis
large handful of fresh blueberries
4 tsp caster sugar
juice of 1 lime
lemonade, soda, tonic water or champagne
   to taste

In the bottom of a cocktail shaker, muddle the blueberries with the sugar and the lime juice using a rolling pin or a wooden pestle. Then add the other ingredients and shake with cubed ice. Strain into tall glasses filled with fresh ice and top with the fizz of your choice.

The quinine in the tonic water together with the fruity bite of the Pimm's makes this a perfect aperitif.

For a blended drink, this is subtle, aromatic and lightly creamy. The saffron is not too overpowering and adds a delicacy to the whole cocktail.

P&T

Serves 1

50 ml/1.5 fl oz Pimm's No. 1 cup
4 strawberries, hulled and chopped (+1 for garnish)
1 tsp caster sugar
juice of 1 lemon
150 ml/5 fl oz tonic water

Put the strawberries in a highball glass with the sugar and crush them together using the end of a rolling pin or a wooden pestle. When the strawberries have been mashed up and the sugar has dissolved, add crushed ice, the lemon juice and Pimm's and top up with tonic water. Garnish with a strawberry.

Southern Silk Route

Serves 2

100 ml/3.5 fl oz vodka
1 pinch saffron threads
2 tbsp caster sugar
4 large strawberries, hulled and halved (+ one for garnish)
100 ml/3.5 fl oz thick Greek yoghurt

In a blender, blend the saffron with the vodka and the sugar (which will make the vodka turn yellow). Then add the strawberries and the yoghurt with some crushed ice and blend together until smooth. Serve in the glasses of your choice, garnished with strawberries.

'When I read about the evils of drinking, I gave up reading.'
Henry Youngman

Easy to make – and even easier to drink.

As the name would suggest, this is a very light, easy drinking, afternoon champagne cocktail.

English Garden
Serves 6

300 ml/10 fl oz gin
900 ml/30 fl oz freshly pressed apple juice
75 ml/2.5 fl oz elderflower cordial
2 limes, cut into wedges

Pour all the ingredients into a large jug and stir well. Fill highball glasses with ice and squeeze the limes into them. Serve at leisure, adding more limes to taste.

Sweetness and Light
Serves 1

1 tbsp orange liqueur
1 tbsp elderflower cordial
1 tbsp freshly squeezed lemon juice
dash Angostura bitters (optional)
champagne
2 strips of lemon peel for garnish

Pour the first four ingredients into a champagne flute and top with champagne. Then zest the oil from the lemon over the surface of the drink.

Tip 10 The best time to polish glasses is when they are still hot and damp. If you are polishing a dry, water-stained glass, hold it upside-down over boiling water for a few seconds. The moisture from the steam loosens any grime and makes polishing much easier. (The lazy option is to pop them in a freezer for half an hour. They get lovely and cold and the frost masks any water stains!)

On the one hand, mysterious, elusive and rich. On the other, tangy, refreshing and dry.

This cocktail is dry and fruity and goes down very easily on hot afternoons.

The Scarlet Pimpernel

Serves 2

75 ml/2.5 fl oz whisky
50 ml/1.5 fl oz crème de cassis
juice of ½ lemon
150 ml/5 fl oz cranberry juice
15 fresh mint leaves (+2 for garnish)

Put the first five ingredients into a cocktail shaker with cubed ice and shake hard. Strain into martini glasses and garnish each one with a mint leaf.

British Summer Time

Serves 6

200 ml/7 fl oz gin
100 ml/3.5 fl oz cherry liqueur
100 ml/3.5 fl oz lime cordial
300 ml/10 fl oz cranberry juice
300 ml/10 fl oz apple juice
juice of 2 lemons
1 lemon, sliced, for garnish

Pour all the ingredients into a jug with the sliced lemon. Mix thoroughly and pour into ice-filled highballs to serve.

'I have taken more out of alcohol than alcohol has taken out of me.' *Winston Churchill*

This classic drink was invented by London bartender Dick Bradsell. It has everything you might expect from a great cocktail and will be around in years to come.

You can't beat the taste of fresh, sweet pineapple... unless of course you add some tequila, lemon and Angostura bitters!

Russian Spring Punch

Serves 2

100 ml/3.5 fl oz vodka
25 ml/1 fl oz crème de cassis
juice of 1 lemon
3 tbsp caster sugar
150 ml/5 fl oz champagne
2 slices of lemon for garnish (optional)

In a cocktail shaker, stir the caster sugar with the lemon juice until it is dissolved then add the vodka and cassis and ice cubes. Shake hard, then strain over fresh ice into two highball glasses. Top up with champagne and garnish each glass with a slice of lemon.

A-Ga-Doo

Serves 2

100 ml/3.5 fl oz tequila
½ ripe pineapple, skinned, cored and cut into
    chunks
2–4 tsp caster sugar (depending on the sweetness of the
    pineapple)
juice of ½ lemon
few dashes of Angostura (optional)
pineapple leaves or chunks of pineapple for
    garnish

Throw all the ingredients (except the garnish) into a blender with a good handful of crushed ice. Blend until thick and pour into tumblers. Garnish with a chunk of the flesh or a couple of leaves.

Booze-free beverages

Just because you are holding the car keys (or are too young to drink alcohol), doesn't mean that you should be missing out on the fun. Here is a selection of delicious drinks to suit all sizes.

A delicious and fruity combination using passion fruit and raspberries.

This is a beautifully fragrant and delicate drink with a lovely sweet/bitter mix coming from the grapefruit and lychee juice.

Party Pooper

Serves 2

20 raspberries (+2 for garnish)
200 ml/7 fl oz passion fruit juice
juice of 1 lime
200 ml/7 fl oz cranberry juice

In a cocktail shaker, shake the ingredients vigorously with cubed ice and then strain into ice-filled highball glasses. Garnish each drink with a raspberry.

Chanel

Serves 2

20 mint leaves (+2 leaves for garnish)
200 ml/7 fl oz lychee juice
200 ml/7 fl oz pink grapefruit juice

Rip the mint leaves into a cocktail shaker, add the juices, then shake with cubed ice and strain into two ice-filled highball glasses. Garnish with a mint leaf.

This is such a good recipe that a jug never hangs around very long.

If you are not very good with alcohol, but don't want to feel left out of a party, this is the drink for you. Peach schnapps is not very alcoholic, so you can quaff a couple of these and still be fine.

Perfectly Peachy Iced Tea

Serves 6

1 litre/32 fl oz boiling water
4 Earl Grey tea bags (or 8 tsp leaf tea)
12 tbsp caster sugar
2 ripe peaches, peeled, stoned and sliced into
    wedges
juice of 1 lemon
lemon slices for garnish

Pour the boiling water and tea bags into a heatproof bowl and leave to steep for no more than 2 minutes. Remove the tea bags and add the sugar, the peaches and the lemon juice, stirring well. When it has cooled enough to go in the fridge, cover it and leave it overnight. Before serving, remove the peach slices and add a further litre/32 fl oz of cold water. Serve in a large jug with ice and slices of lemon.

Donkey Ride (low alcohol)

Serves 1

25 ml/1 fl oz peach schnapps
1 whole lime, cut into eight
150 ml/5 fl oz grapefruit juice
50 ml/1.5 fl oz ginger beer

In the bottom of a highball glass, crush the lime using the end of a rolling pin or a wooden pestle. Then add cubed ice, the grapefruit juice and the peach schnapps. Top up with ginger beer.

This is a sweet, fragrant, yet slightly bitter drink.

To make good iced coffee you really need to use proper espresso, but you can get away with just making a very strong filter or cafetière coffee.

Kiwi Crush

Serves 4

1 ripe kiwi, peeled and sliced
50 ml/1.5 fl oz elderflower cordial
500 ml/16 fl oz grapefruit juice

Chuck the kiwi into a blender until it has puréed, (see 'How to' page 110) then either throw the other ingredients in and blend with crushed ice, or transfer the mixture to an ice-filled cocktail shaker and shake with the other ingredients. Strain into ice-filled highball glasses and garnish with two thin slices of kiwi.

Iced Coffee Deluxe

Serves 2

1 double espresso
3 scoops vanilla ice cream
250 ml/8.5 fl oz semi-skimmed milk
4 tsp caster sugar

Put all the ingredients into a blender with a handful of crushed ice and whizz until smooth. Pour into two tall glasses and serve.

Tropical and healthy – you might need thick straws to suck up all that goodness.

What a healthy way to start the day – a classic Virgin Mary with V8. Alternatively, if you have a hangover, then try this with a splash of vodka – just add a little more Worcestershire sauce.

Jungle Boogie
Serves 2

1 whole mango (peeled, stone removed and flesh chopped)
fresh pineapple (about 2.5 cm/1 inch long), peeled and chopped
1 banana (you guessed it, peeled and chopped)
mango slices for garnish (optional)

Chuck the lot into a blender with lots of ice and whiz until thick and smooth. Serve in tall glasses. If you want to make it look at bit special, then garnish with two slices of mango.

V8 Virgin
Serves 2

500 ml/16 fl oz V8 vegetable juice
1 tbsp Worcestershire sauce
5 dashes of Tabasco
juice of ½ lemon
pinch of salt
grind of black pepper
½ tsp creamed horseradish
2 celery sticks for garnish (optional)

Shake everything together except the garnish with cubed ice and strain into ice-filled highball glasses. Garnish with the celery sticks if you want.

This recipe was shown to me by a palm reader in India. This is how the Indians drink tea – which seems strange, but it is rich and subtle. It is a great warming drink if the weather is cold and wet outside. I like to use the blend called Breakfast Tea in this drink.

A very dry and slightly bitter libation to get the gastric juices flowing before dinner.

My Chai

Tea for 3

350 ml/12 fl oz milk
3 thin slices fresh root ginger
2 tea bags (or 4 tsp leaf tea)
4 tsp caster sugar

In a pan over a medium heat, heat the milk with the ginger. Before it starts boiling add the tea and sugar. When it starts to bubble and foam up, remove the pan from the heat. Repeat twice until the milk has darkened. Strain off any loose tea, ginger and skin from the milk and serve in teacups.

Gandhi's Flip-Flop

Serves 1

juice of ½ lemon
juice of ½ orange
1 tsp caster sugar
200 ml/7 fl oz tonic water
wedge of lemon or a slice of orange for garnish (optional)

Fill a tall glass with ice and stir in the first four ingredients. Garnish the drink with lemon or orange if you want.

Not one of my inventions, but a hugely popular drink in Australia. A great balance of flavours and perfect refreshment when the sun is blazing down.

Deliciously thick and lightly creamy.

Lemonade, Lime & Bitters
Serves 1

200 ml/7 fl oz lemonade
3–5 dashes Angostura bitters
juice of ½ lime
wedge of lime

Fill a highball glass with cubed ice and add the lemonade, bitters and lime juice. Stir well, then squeeze the lime wedge into the drink and drop it in.

Sweet Sixteen
Serves 2

2 whole peaches, stoned and sliced
10 strawberries, hulled and sliced
2 tbsp caster sugar
100 ml/3.5 fl oz water
100 ml/3.5 fl oz single cream

Put all the ingredients into a blender with a handful of crushed ice and blend until smooth and slushy. Serve in wine glasses.

A lovely dry and summery concoction for catching rays in the garden.

You can also use tropical juices such as coconut and pineapple juice in this drink, although you may need to add fresh lime juice to add a sour note to the sweeter juices.

No Sex Please, We're British

Serves 4

50 ml/1.5 fl oz elderflower cordial
500 ml/16 fl oz cranberry juice
500 ml/16 fl oz apple juice
2 limes, chopped into wedges
mint sprigs for garnish (optional)

Throw the first three ingredients into a large jug filled with ice, then squeeze the limes into it and stir. Serve in highball glasses. If you have any mint, then add a sprig to each drink for extra freshness.

Mango Lassi

Serves 2

2 tbsp natural or Greek yoghurt
300 ml/10 fl oz mango juice

In a cocktail shaker, shake both ingredients hard with cubed ice and strain into ice-filled highball glasses.

How to...

In this chapter I explain the finer points and details of making drinks, from puréeing fruit to making sugar syrup.

Unfortunately, if you don't have a blender/liquidizer, you won't be able to make any blended drinks. The art of getting a smooth, icy drink is the proportion of ice to liquid (which is normally about one third ice to two thirds liquid) and how much fruit you use to thicken it with. The end result should be a little like soft ice cream. Ideally, crushed ice should be used as this saves the blades on your blender and eases the smoothness of the drink.

If in doubt, add the ice slowly when the blender is running. If the drink gets 'stiff' and doesn't blend, then you have put too much ice in. Some blenders have ice crushing capabilities, but check before you chuck in cubed ice as you will ruin your blender. If you have chunks of fruit or large cubes of ice, then use the pulse switch and do few short fast actions to break up the big bits. If you have a speed control setting, then start at the slowest speeds and end on the fastest. It should take between 30 seconds and one minute to fully blend a drink.

The best way is to use an ice-crushing machine or one of the larger blenders which have strong blades for ice crushing. If you don't have either, fret not!

Take a clean plastic carrier bag and place a couple of handfuls of fresh, dry ice inside it (half-melted ice does not work very well). Then wrap a dry tea towel around the plastic making it look something like an ice pack (good for bruises). Using the bottom of a bottle or a rolling pin, smash up the ice, turning the towel so that it crushes evenly. (Be careful what surface you use to smash it on – wooden surfaces will dent.) Voilà! You now have perfectly crushed ice and all your stress and tension have suddenly vanished!

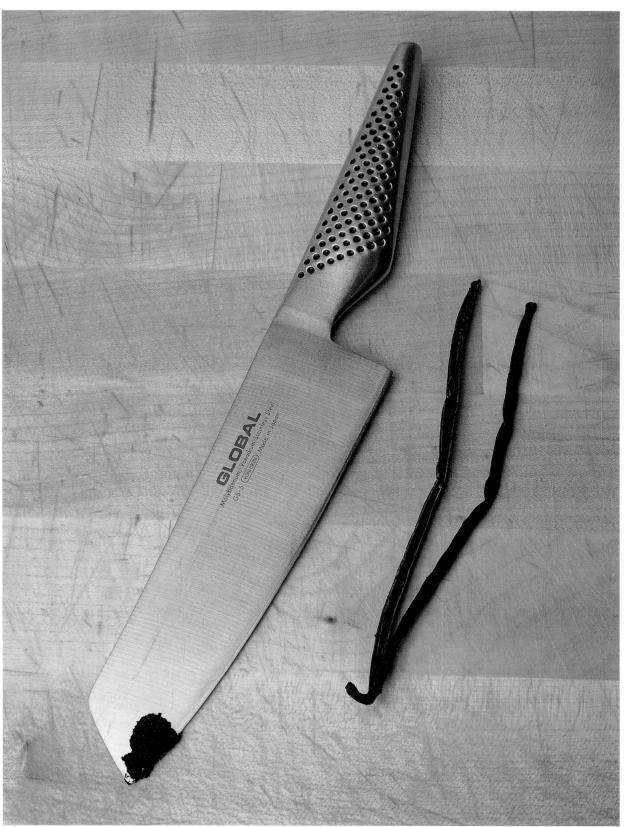

You can infuse herbs, fruits and spices in virtually any spirits although the best results are achieved by using complementary flavours. For example, whiskies, rum, cognac and bourbon have natural and subtle vanilla notes which come from being aged in wooden barrels. By infusing vanilla into these brown spirits, it exaggerates the natural flavour and gives you a more punchy flavour.

To infuse vanilla into a spirit using a whole vanilla pod, take a sharp knife and split the pod lengthways. Then lay the pod down and, holding one end, use the edge of the knife to scrape out the small black seeds. Then just put the pod and the seeds into the bottle and leave in a warm place for a few days (you can leave the vanilla in there as long as you want and it will continue to flavour it). The more vanilla pods you put in, the more intense the vanilla flavour. If you want to drink the spirit neat, then add about 15–30 ml/1–2 tablespoons of light brown sugar with the vanilla. Other ingredients which can be used to flavour brown spirits are cinnamon, raisins, cloves and star anise.

Although fresh fruits can be used for infusions, they go brown and nasty looking and it is better to add these at the time you make the drinks. Herbs and spices always work the best.

Vodka is the best spirit to use when infusing flavours because it is almost neutral. It is like working with a blank canvas and any mixture of flavours can be added.

To make home-made lemon vodka, peel a lemon (try not to get any of the white pith on the peel as this will make the vodka bitter) and put the peel into a bottle of vodka. It will start flavouring as soon as it goes into the spirit and will carry on until you take it out. (If you leave the lemon peel in the bottle for longer than, roughly, two months, the flavours will get very intense and the peel will discolour). You can also use orange or lime peel, lemongrass, ginger, chilli, and all kinds of dried spices.

Under no circumstances (unless being ironic) should umbrellas, sparklers, or plastic monkeys be used to garnish drinks. If you have made a good drink and served it in a nice clean glass, then most drinks don't need a garnish. Even if you are trying to impress, I am a firm believer that less is more.

Use garnishes sparingly and use them in proportion to the glass. I think that the garnish that you use for a drink should be part of the drink itself. Thus, the dusting of cinnamon over 'The Voodoo' (page 33) not only looks appealing, it also finishes the taste and smell of the drink. The same is said for the lemon twist on a classic martini (page 46) because even though you don't eat the peel, the oil from the citrus skin leaves a sweet zestiness over the drink. Huge slices of pineapple with cherries stuck in them are a thing of the past and should be forgotten (along with leather ties that have piano keys printed on them).

Making your own fruit purée means that you can make the same cocktails over and over again with minimal effort (and you can freeze it so that you only have to go to the effort of making the purée once).

Some fruits purée more easily than others. Raspberries, for example, just need to be thrown into a liquidizer/blender and blitzed until smooth. Other fruits, such as peaches, need a little water added for lubrication and sometimes also a little caster sugar to bring out their natural sweetness. Some fruits need to be peeled or have the flesh cut away from the stone (mangoes) but the results are very satisfying. When you purée fruit, the end result should be thick and sweet, not watery and tasteless – remember that fruit at the beginning and end of the season will never be that great. Fruit purée will last in the fridge in a tightly covered container for a number of days, but the best way to make sure that it stays fresh is to freeze it. This also means you can make fruit-based cocktails when the fruits are out of season. A great way is to freeze the purée into an ordinary ice-cube tray. Just take it out of the freezer about an hour before you need it.

The following fruits all make good purées as they are fleshy and do not have large pips: bananas, blackberries, blueberries, kiwis, mangoes, melons, strawberries and peaches.

Tip 12
When zesting the surface of drinks with citrus peel, use lemons or limes that are hard and unripe. They are easier to peel and spray out loads of pungent zest when squeezed (see page 116 for more details)

The quality of fruit that is available to you will vary greatly depending on where you live. The most important fruits in cocktail-making are the citrus ones and these are the ones that vary the most in sweetness and quantity of juice. Limes, for example, often come into supermarkets hard and only start to ripen when you get them home.

The cycle of lemons and limes ripening is like this: Unripe, they may look a good colour, but they start off very hard and with very little bitter juice inside. Left in the sun for a few days, they will soften up a treat. When lemons and limes go squidgy and soft to the touch then they are perfect. They will be much easier to squeeze and you will get loads of juice out of them. If you leave limes even longer, their skins go really tough and they start to go brown – best to use them before this happens. Lemons just start to grow mould.

Dealing with unripe citrus fruit: if you only have unripe fruit to hand, one useful trick is to roll them as hard as you can on a work surface under the palm of your hand. This loosens any juice inside the fruit and helps when you come to squeeze them. If you have lots to squeeze, then leaving them to soak in hot water for five minutes has a similar effect.

Fruit facts

- *Oranges, lemons, limes and grapefruit are at their juiciest when soft to the touch.*

- *An average lime contains 30–45 ml (2–3 tbsp) juice and a lemon between 30–75 ml (2–5 tbsp).*

- *Ripe peaches should be firm to the touch, but will have a little give to them when you touch the flesh. If the skin appears loose or slightly wrinkly, then they are on the turn.*

- *Mangoes should also have good tight skin, but should be quite soft and smell ripe.*

- *Ripe watermelon should give a deep, hollow sound when tapped and will have a good pattern over the surface.*

- *All berries should be plump and rich in colour.*

- *Ripe bananas are mottled with 50 per cent brown over the yellow skin.*

- *Ripe passion fruit should be the size of a small egg and should be slightly wrinkly. When they start to shrink and get very wrinkly, they are past their best.*

How to... Use sugar

In the recipes in this book I use either caster sugar or light soft brown sugar (sometimes called muscovado). Both dissolve into liquids much easier than granulated sugar. Any recipes containing sugar specify that it should be dissolved first. The reason for this is that sugar dissolves much more easily into citrus juice and room-temperature alcohol than anything else. Sugar can, of course, be added to a drink when it is cold – it will just take longer to dissolve. I tend to use brown sugar when I am using brown spirits, as the taste of molasses complements the richness of the aged spirit.

How to... Make sugar syrup
Professional bars use sugar syrup or *syrop de gomme*, which is a mix of sugar, water (and, often, other flavourings such as orange blossom or E-numbers). In this book, I mostly use caster sugar, because I find it easy and convenient to use, but if you are planning to set up a semi-professional home bar, then use the sugar syrup recipe below and substitute the caster sugar in the following ratio:

15 ml (1 tbsp) caster sugar = 25 ml sugar syrup

15 ml (1 tbsp) caster sugar = 5 tsp sugar syrup

To make 1 litre/32 fl oz sugar syrup, slowly stir together 500 ml/16 fl oz water and 900 g (2 lb) caster sugar in a saucepan over medium heat. When the liquid starts to bubble and boil, immediately reduce the heat and stir just until all the sugar has dissolved. Leave it to cool completely and bottle it.

How to... Make vanilla sugar
Vanilla sugar is great for all kinds of cocktails and baking. It gives drinks another mellow and aromatic dimension and works particularly well with brown spirits. You can buy ready-made vanilla sugar in some supermarkets, although it is very easy to make yourself. Take 250 g/9 oz caster sugar and one whole vanilla pod. Hold one end of the vanilla pod and slice down the centre. Use the side of the knife blade and scrape out the little black seeds. When all the seeds have been scraped out, cut the pod into smaller pieces and, in a bowl, mix the seeds, bits of pod and sugar together. It is now ready to use, but the flavour will increase the longer it is in there. Keep in the cupboard in a jar with a tight screw top. Don't eat the pods! They don't digest very well.

Tip 13 If you are using premium-strength spirits (more than 40 per cent ABV/80 degrees proof) to make your cocktails, you may find that you need to add more sugar to the recipe to balance the extra alcohol.

With many of my recipes, I finish the drink with a piece of citrus zest which sprays the oil from the peel of the fruit onto the surface of the drink, making a lovely, aromatic smell before you put the glass to your lips. Lemon zest, in particular, helps bring out the flavours of the drink and gives cocktails a little more sophistication.

The best way to prepare citrus zest is to use a vegetable peeler to cut off just the thin peel (the white pith underneath is bitter and should be left behind). Be careful, for if you squeeze the peel before aiming, you will lose all those lovely oils. Then take the strip of peel (zest) between your thumb and forefinger and, in one motion, squeeze the zest over the surface of the freshly made drink to release the oil (this is called zesting). If the light is right, you should be able to see a thin spray of oil coming off it. For best results, use lemons that are hard and slightly unripe.

When making drinks to take to the park/beach/sailing, etc. the liquid will stay hot or cold longer if you fill the flask with cold or hot water first.

It's very simple: for chilled drinks, just put a handful of ice cubes in the flask and top up with cold water. Gently rock it backwards and forwards to chill it down. Discard the cold water and fill with prepared drink of choice. It's the same for hot drinks, only use hot water.

Throughout this book I work in millilitres and also give the equivalent in fluid ounces. With some recipes I have rounded up or down by a few ml, just to 'tidy up' the recipes a little.

 1 tsp (teaspoon) = 5 ml = ⅙ fl oz

1 tbsp (tablespoon) = 15 ml = ½ fl oz

Shot (UK) = 25 ml

Pony (US) = 29.5 ml = 1 fl oz

Egg cup = 25 ml (average)

Advantix film case = 25 ml

35mm film case = 35 ml

Juice of a lemon = 30–75 ml/1–2.5 fl oz

Juice of a lime = 30–50 ml/1–1.5 fl oz

What can I do with...?

A
Advocaat: Canary, p21
Amaretto: St. Germain, p42; Godfather, p69

B
Brandy (or Cognac): Light My Fire, p31; French Daiquiri, p41; St. Germain, p.42; Grassyarse senõr, p57; Blood, Sweat and Sand, p54; Hot-Digidy-Chocolate, p58; French Toddy, p60; Ginger Snap, p59; Big Baby Milk, p65; Two's a Pear, p68; AK Cold Relief, p67; The Kiwi, p76
Bourbon: Bloody Mary-Lou, p18; American Breakfast, p51; Bourbon Beach Iced Tea, p60; Tennessee Travel Companion, p59; Hot-Digidy-Chocolate, p58; Hot Bourbon with Marmalade, p65; Spicy Mash, p70; Old Fashioned, p67
Basil: Mediterranean Martini, p45; Ruby Tuesday, p82
Banana (fresh): Jungle Boogie, p100
Blueberries: Blueberry Sling, p83
Blackberries: Diablo Jelly, p29; Blackberry Collins, p76

C
Campari: Ignorance is Bliss, p44
Champagne: Rosso Royale, p21; Coal Cliff Bellini, p27; Pear and Elderflower Bellini, p27; Love Soane, p31; Persian Prince, p37; Champagne and Pink Grapefruit Granita, p42; Russian Spring Punch, p91; Sweetness and Light, p87; Blueberry Sling, p83
Crème de Cassis: Hokey Cokey, p26; Bloody Breeze, p33; Blood, Sweat and Sand, p54; French Toddy, p60; Russian Spring Punch, p91; Scarlet Pimpernel, p88; Blueberry Sling, p83
Cider: Hot Spiced Cider, p64
Coconut cream: Blizzard, p22; Be-a Substitute, p36
Coffee: Vodka Espresso, p41; Irish Coffee, p64; Iced Coffee Deluxe, p98
Cherry Brandy: Light My Fire, p31; Scottish Sweetheart, p68; British Summer Time, p88
Chocolate: Light My Fire, p31; Hot-Digidy-Chocolate, p58
Clementines: Mexican Breakfast, p38
Cucumber: Two Inches of Cucumber, p45; Park Life, p57
Cream: St. Germain, p42; Sweet Sixteen, p102

D
Dry Vermouth: Dry Martini, p46

E
Elderflower Cordial: GE&T, p50; English Garden, p87; Sweetness and Light, p87; No Sex Please, We're British, p103; Kiwi Crush, p98

G
Gin: Pomegranita, p22; Gin Jelly, p29; Love Soane, p31; Jasmine Punch, p48; Colonial Conclusion, p36; Mediterranean Martini, p45; GE&T, p50; The Limey, p50; British Summer Time, p88; St. Clements Crush, p81; English Garden, p87; Ruby Tuesday, p76; Blackberry Collins, p82
Ginger beer: Blockbuster, p30; Donkey Ride, p97
Ginger (Fresh): Easy Tiger, p48; Mango No. 5, p49; Ginger Snap, p59; Kiss My Peach, p75; My Chai, p101
Guava juice: Unlikely Marriage, p49; Lotus Flower, p46
Grapes: Mediterranean Martini, p45
Grape juice: Park Life, p57

H
Honey: Spicy Mash, p70; Hot Spiced Cider, p64; Easy Tiger, p48; AK Cold Relief, p67

J
Jelly: Gin Jelly, p29; Diablo Jelly, p29

K
Kiwi (fresh): The Kiwi, p82; Kiwi Crush, p98

L
Lager: Dandy Shandy, p51
Lychee juice: Chanel, p94

M
Mint: Mojito, p18; Scarlet Pimpernel, p88; Chanel, p94
Melon: Senõrita, p38
Mango (fresh): Jungle Boogie, p100
Mango juice: Mango No. 5, p49; Totally Tropical, p79; Mango Lassi, p103

Thank you to everyone who has got involved in this book on a personal level, especially to hat-trick, the designers who let me and Martin into their homes with a camera to take pictures of their families. Thank you guys for having faith and patience in the project – the book looks great! Cheers also to Michael and Fiona and C.P. Hart in Lambeth for letting us use their swanky kitchens, the man who let us onto his barge to shoot, the two tramps who we made drink Martinis and last but not least, my girlfriend, Nicola who is a constant source of inspiration and cocktail names! Thank you for your 'constructive criticism' and support. Love you.

About the author...

Alex Kammerling comes from a long line of teetotalers, but is managing to slowly catch up. He has been bartending for over 10 years and has won various cocktail competitions and prizes. He has worked in bars in Sydney and Hong Kong, but his last full-time bar position was in legendary cocktail bar Detroit, in London's Covent Garden. He now works for IP Bartenders mixing drinks at celebrity parties, writing for various magazines such as *Class* and *Square Meal* and trains bartenders about spirits and how to mix them. He is 28 and lives in East London.

About the photographer...

Martin Langfield graduated from the London College of Printing with a degree in graphic design as a fresh-faced 21-year-old. He started assisting well-known photographers soon after college and set-up his own photography business a few years after that. He now has 21 years experience behind him and has shot everything from still life to road-kill. In the last 10 years Martin has been heavily involved in shooting drinks brands and has worked on Stolichnaya, Martini, Famous Grouse and Macallan. Some of Martin's signature work can be seen in the current Bombay Sapphire advertising campaign.